SOCIAL MEDIA: SOCIALLY MEDIOCRE

POEMS ABOUT THE EFFECTS OF SOCIAL MEDIA
BY MISAEL TRUJILLO

Dear Miz,

You asked me to write you a foreword. But I also wanted to write you a thank-you letter.

In your poems, you cover mental health and social media-induced isolation with the kind of brutal honesty that only exists between a patient and their therapist. If the sentiments were any more real, I'd have cut my hand just turning the page. My delight in the artistry was matched only by my discomfort with the subject matter because these issues, to a greater or lesser extent, affect everyone I know.

In the age of insecurity and obfuscated posturing, your courage in confronting your demons shows that for men to be men, they need only to be human first.

My hope is that people will pass these poems on, attend your performances, and start having their own conversations and epiphanies about how their online life is strangling their offline life.

Yours with love, kindness, and compassion.

Emma

Foreword

I first met Miz a number of years ago, as the new boyfriend of my cherished friend Jayne. He came across as a friendly guy with a shy smile and an easy laugh.

I thought I knew the man - as a talented musician, as Jayne's creative and loving partner, and as a friend. It turns out that like most friends of people that suffer with anxiety, I didn't know the half of it.

Miz's creative chops speak for themselves and make a list too long to print. As well as working in the creative industries, over the last ten years when not touring extensively across the UK and Europe with bands or releasing vinyl under No Panic & Local Colour Records, Miz DJ'd regular Indie nights in London as well as for festivals. Miz's background in the raw authenticity of live performance has certainly been influential in his relationship with social media - to go from the honesty of performing live on stage to the polished disingenuousness of social media is to go from a warm fireside into a freezing wasteland.

These poems have a relentless pace and cadence that leave me breathless every time. The work pulses with a defiant beat that grants no quarter - neither for the false opiate that is social media, nor Miz himself.

This is an important and articulate work by a young man who in trying his hardest to be better, can help us all be better.

Miz's courage in confronting toxic masculinity and social anxiety is not only admirable but the work - mother of god! The **work**, the **words** and the **rhythm** have a proportion that belongs only to great artists.

Please pass this work on to others whom you think might benefit. Lives have depended on less.

Emma Jackson - Digital & UX Consultant/Entrepreneur

Turn off notifications, sit back, relax and enjoy.

Happy, Happy, Happy

I woke up
upset
at a series of events that
can not
be put
to rest

they wouldn't sit there like a chip on my shoulder
so I paced round the house like a mighty boulder

I told myself to chill
to show some rational
not to let dickheads get me down

they're just drinking their beers
just smoking it up
living their perfect fucking lives
every perfect fucking night
whilst I'm sitting at home
soaking it up
thinking I'm some kind of cursed man
with some filthy rotten luck
when really it's unhealthy for my brain
to pretend my friends are happy
happy
happy
when really
they're not

it was that conclusion
that gave me piece of mind
then tore my mind to pieces
as I tried to piece together
the so called friends
that make me feel like living is a crime

yet I yearn for their likes

I feed off their comments

I base my perception of succeeding

on their moronic achievements
get pissed off and say I have no freedom
I'm enslaved by a community of peers
who only let me peer into their friendship system
systematically keeping their distance
automatically assuming
I'm the obvious resistance
to their somehow
perfect
system

Origin Story

I can't quite remember if Hi5 or Bebo came first
but I recall the hope
that maybe friendships would be
easier than before

climbing the social ladder
was already the ultimate chore

by the time MySpace was "in"
I'd realised nothing had changed
the same rules that applied in life
applied online, remaining unchanged

we don't become social
because you call it social media
in fact
we dig deeper

some people found it easy
as easy as a stroll through life
others found it tough
like using a blunt shaving knife

I became aware of
how lonely I really was

but I can't turn it off

Morning Routine

I tend to wake up
turn on Facebook
shuffle around until I find a comfy nook
lay there in bed
surfing the web
wishing I could be bothered to read a book

Change

constant change
I want the same
just don't have the energy to constantly sway

there's days I wake up
hug the floor.
attempt to pray.
"dear God I hope it all stays this way"

then there's weeks that I hate the way I behave
constantly observing other people change

I want to be vegan and cruelty free
I want to start running and I want to see
Hawaii
Peru
Ho Chi Minh City

I want to read more
tour more
be more
sleep less
earn more
work less
buy more
own less
stop my brain from feeling like a mess

I want to be kinder
to others and myself

I want to get round to finally putting up that shelf
I saw you buy at IKEA

I wasn't stalking.
though …
if I'm being sincere

Instagram Filter

turning on the screen
burns my eyes with raging flames
stinks of jealousy

Faith In Society

it nevers stops

I still see it scroll through as I close my eyes

a constant stream of meaningless shares and likes

fake caring

losing identity to become the wanted archetype

a complete and utter stereotype

and I don't mean to generalise because
I've been stereotyped before

being Spanish I get the obvious
"Ey Matador"
having a siesta?
good on the dance floor?
when's the next fiesta?

all that shit I try and ignore
but the crap that you share on your stream
like a precise breakdown of what exactly you wore
to your mate's birthday bash during spring
leaves me
not just bored to the core
… but raw

Facebook Turns Opinion Into Bullshit

rational speech and belief
the two don't always seem to fit
I'm talking full on punch up in the street
black eye and a fat lip

see, as humans we're proud beings
quick to turn words into machetes
forget everything we ever knew about sportsmanship
have kids round?
shout a big FUCK YOU to censorship

when it comes to what we believe
there's no bargaining chip
civilized gentlemen turn into football hooligans
godly men into hypocrites
only just realising they're on a sinking ship

and it's mainly privileged upper class atheists
who I watch in this position
mouths foaming
down on all fours
fighting for dominion

trying to use their opinion
to cause an incision
at the very least a division
between themselves and who they consider, what?
competition?
the opposition?
someone who just follows their family's tradition?

stop shoving down other people's throats
your own uneducated opinions
you regurgitate them badly
and none of us are your bloody minions

Post It Note To Self

if awake at night
please avoid the internet

my friend Matt taught me
to love myself more than that
and when I use it
I feel like a hypocrite

Cyber Relationships

put up your drinks
put on your grins
it's time to make a show
because being down is so two years ago
it's not "in" in this town

I get the hint
I'll lock myself away
try to justify my reasons for wanting out of this machine

I've been biting tongues
trying to find a cure for breaking bones
using misspoken words
or never speaking them at all

I've been fucking up more than you care to admit
but the fact is admitting
has never come easy to me

if we could just talk face to face
I think you might agree
that all this pointless bullshit
is the cause of nothing but greed

I want to see the world
I want people to see me
I want everyone to be my friend
without taking my eye off the screen

Spanish Subtitles

I heard your call
I was just too afraid to answer

I heard the phone
I was frozen to the sofa

I heard your call
and it gave me no hope at all
I heard the phone
I hate my own voice
so I was frozen with fear on the sofa

because I can never sense
when the time's right to talk
I can never sense
when the time's right at all
I can never sense
when the time's right to talk
so cease

oh I heard your call

I tried to intertwine thoughts and wine
to make some witty comment

I heard the phone
but every time I try to speak
I feel like I might vomit

I heard your call
it gave me no hope at all
I heard the phone
but I hate my own voice
so if I try and speak I feel like I might vomit

Conversation With Father

turn
that
racket
down
you know I'm not amused

I miss sitting 'round listening to the news
I miss my best friend
miss my son
miss the drives where we'd talk about your mum

I need advice
need new tunes
need some space, just me and you
miss cleaning windows and talking about God
need some confirmation of what I am worth
as a father and son

as a husband
as a best friend
as a God fearing man

and who do I complain to now?
who do I complain to now?

I stole hope from a hospital room
the night you were born
but who do I complain to now?

Dear Screen

dear screen
please rip me apart at the seams
I need to get used to the feeling
of falling asleep

Stranger

you thought I was strange
so I turned into a stranger
but how can I not be strange
when I have friends like you?

like you give a damn who I am
or what I become
what fucking mixer I drink with my rum
how many likes you got on your insta
the fact your second cousin had a new sister
her name, her weight, her security number
I got to know you better than family

you
a stranger
who thought I was strange
made me feel so self conscious I had to go shave
simply because you decided to comment that day

you
who made me feel strange

Fading

washed up
but not afraid

this box has made me lose my faith

I know I'm not far away
and though it's only space
I beg you don't come round tonight

I've crashed my user interface

too much staring at a cube
googling "capillary tube"
reading up on pointless news
missing out on verbal cues

I feel like I no longer talk
and I do this round the clock
just type away into a box

so ... detox

I'm washed up
but not afraid
this box has made me lose my voice
but it hasn't sealed my fate

Introducing Myself To A Facebook Group

I'm feeling nervous about this
you see I've never done it before
what have I let myself in for?

I've got a story to tell
but I've always been afraid to tell it
keep getting distracted by metaphors
I've memorised from watching telly
cliches I convince myself are good for my mental health
whilst staying up at night
wishing I didn't have to put up with this hell

I was good at speaking once
face to face
hated talking on the phone
talking is always a race
let's see who types fastest
out of a hundred people I don't even know

so I'm feeling nervous about this
because I've always felt nervous in groups
then the group became a sea of people
and I'm constantly expecting them to take the piss

Questions On The Internet

I'm tired of answering questions on the internet

they're often asked by strangers
who I guess don't realise they can Google it

to me it seem completely absurd
but regardless of the stupidity
people seem undeterred

going to the beach, should I get my hair wet?
heading to Peru, just wondering if there's many dangers?

is it technically safe to bury your head in a sand pit?

how much money should I put on this bet?
should I get in this blacked out car with strangers?
how exactly do I go about getting a work permit?

what's the best way to cook a baguette?
who's the latest player booked for the Rangers?
should I get a ridiculous tattoo done on my armpit?

they want the answer given to them word for word
with no friendship, handshake
or thank you incurred

it seems completely absurd
but regardless of the stupidity
people seem undeterred

Lost & Found

I'm tired
put me in a box
write a note that says

wake me up when the world's a kinder place

for goodness sake
has it really been five years since I last prayed?

doesn't seem much of a point

feed me money on a plate
I got a new camera
shoots 4K
all my fans agree it's fucking A
I think I deserve some shelter from the rain
some relief from the pain

if I were born poor
it would obviously be another way

what kind of a prick do you take me for anyway?

just chuck me in the lost and found
I'd rather be lost than found
when there's this shit going around
just chuck me in the lost and found
I'll be found when there's some more hope around

You Bring The Beers

last year I almost broke
only one person caught my fall
so I had a go at self-esteem
I mean
they all clearly saw me break
it's just easier to tilt the screen

it's easier to talk shit
bring the beers
come and hang
easier to talk shit

we're talking thirteenth floor
feet over the ledge
no hope

you come and hang and bring the beers
you bring the beers
you bring the beers
leave as I break
you bring the beers
you come and hang
and bring the beers

it's just easier to talk shit
bring the beers
come and hang
talk shit

Are You And Your Online Presence A Couplet?

did you really spend all day
swiping the screen & feeling this way?

you really think enough scrolling through the web
will somehow miraculously turn you into a celeb?

millions of subscribers don't mean a thing
when instead of creating you're hanging by a string
when instead of living you're dating your screen
and spending your time complaining

E-Bank Balance

my bank emailed me my balance this morning

I used to be able to put it off
until I wanted to feel crap
remind myself of my low worth
spend some time searching crap jobs
reading up self-help blogs
that just make me want to own more
make me feel less secure
less good looking
less adored
more like the person I once feared
BORED

The People Who Matter

Jayne, for always being by my side and for everything else in between.

Emma Jackson, for somehow finding time and for inspiring both Jayne & me.

Richard Heaven, for his advice, his time and for keeping it real. I'm glad we haven't lost touch.

Jonny Gill, for being an exemplary human being.

David Ricardo Santana Crawford, for becoming my brother and always taking the time.

To Mat Callaghan, without you I'd probably have grown up already, I can't wait to come visit you in Myanmar.

To Damaris, my sister, for being strong, for being brave and inspiring me to be better.

To Lee and the rest of Larkhill through the years, because playing music with you was keeping me sane.

To my Mum and Dad, who will probably never see this, but whom I love very much.

To anyone who takes time out of their day to read these words.

Thank you, from the bottom of my heart.

Misael Trujillo.

P.S. It didn't seem fitting to include social media handles or websites in this book, for very obvious reasons. However, that doesn't mean we can't be found. I'm sure if you were inclined to pick up this book, you already know how to find me.